# pulse

# pulse

*poems by*
Rajinderpal S. Pal

ARSENAL
PULP PRESS
*Vancouver*

PULSE

ARSENAL PULP PRESS
103-1014 Homer Street
Vancouver, B.C.
Canada v6B 2w9
*arsenalpulp.com*

The publisher gratefully acknowledges the support of
the Canada Council for the Arts and the British Columbia
Arts Council for its publishing program, and the Government of Canada
through the Book Publishing Industry Development Program
for its publishing activities.

Book and cover design by Solo
Cover photographs by Arion Predika
Printed and bound in Canada

NATIONAL LIBRARY OF CANADA
CATALOGUING IN PUBLICATION DATA:
Pal, Rajinderpal S.
Pulse

ISBN 1-55152-130-X

I. Title.
PS8581.A486P84 2002    C811'.54    C2002-911016-5

PR9199.3.P315P84 2002

*for sukhpal*

Oh how we want to be
taken and changed, want
to be mended by
what we enter.

– Jorie Graham

# I

# that childhood language

I

the past is another country
            in another language, the way
you cup lentils in your hand
            funnel them into water
how you measure salt
            in the dent of your palm
or pick a pea-pod
            between thumb and index finger
let it fall into the *chuni*
            gathered at your waist


you never speak of love
            only the learning: the folding of dough
and *thodka* – what everything begins with
            a recipe; an address
a scrap of paper folded and folded again
            into the pocket of your petticoat
a direction home, a letter
            you had others read to you
your hands the colour of turmeric
            cotton thread around bittermelons

you never speak of love
        as though to talk is an extraction
the spirit in the camera
        the ghost in the well
and there are other silences you keep
        your childhood home
expired sisters
        what of your mother?
your father?
        widowhood?
the lost child?
        these shifts across continents and language?


and now you document
        how those around you have passed on
a list of cancers; the sugar illness
        and traffic accidents
the coke can under the brake pedal
        the *chuni* caught on the spokes of a bicycle wheel
and what they left undone or incomplete
        siblings without passage or children unmarried


the past is an enormous shadow
        over cracked walls
thrown by a kerosene lamp
        in a pink plastered room
where we hovered over each other
        like locust clouds
no question of privacy or option
        no question of desire

*the devout measure their lives*
*in denial and forgetting*
*conjure ways of forgiving*
*to keep on living*


that other language offered
            the possibility of relief
a chance the rain
            would settle the dust
for another journey another year; the earth
            its endless mending and re-mending
now that other place is
            a poem in a book or a photograph


*all writing is apology*
*that is not what i meant to say*
*this is not how i meant to say it*


the written word was always
            a high window
dust in a shaft of light
            strangers with faces covered
on a rope bed on the rooftop
            we counted stars
and the silver in your hair
            you said the stars were bits of daylight
pin-holes in a black box
            nothing instead of something

## II

you were sixteen
        and the groom still in the army
so you sat next to a photograph
        in your red and gold suit
and you circled four times
            a black and white of a turbaned soldier


for months he never touched you
        returned from war
knowing distance through a lens
        the scoop of earth for a land-mine
camouflage in jungle
          he had never held anyone not bleeding


it was you who took his hand
        placed it over your breast
he felt the pulse
        and the young girl beneath
and when you bled
        it was then he held you


you learned love in the time it took
        your father-in-law
to irrigate the fields
        slats of wood lifted
water through a maze
        of burrowed ground

the time it took
          your mother-in-law
to travel to a nearby *pind*
          one hand on a bundle of food
the other holding her *chuni* over her face
          dust and strangers


or love in the sepia light of morning
          in a mustard field
the smell and taste of *nim* on your mouths
          shoulders, forearms, midriffs
the smell of sleep
          sweat and mustard


> *all writing is fiction*
> *you keep everything inside*
> *unwilling to burden others*
> *with what you most desire to unburden*


never a question of privacy
          or the option to turn away
love as unquestionable
          as water from a well
starch in men's shirts and turbans
          loyalty and duty

through your children you learned
those indirect passages
connecting hands through a child
legs lifted in air
or a glass of water carried by tiny hands
from one to the other


when your first child died
you waited
for another daughter
gave her the same name
spent months awake at her bedside
just in case

## III

you refused to meet her
        and i had no words to convince you
you talked of duty
        of the failure of one who dies
without completion; the one hand
        cleaning the other
that love was something private
        the eyeball its imperfect socket


to begin to describe
        every ridge of vertebra
the soft hair that lined them
        shadow of window-blinds imposed on her body
the strain and the arch
        the restrain the push
the skin and teeth
        how we would braid and unbraid


to sleep with one arm curved over
        hand stretched hard against her belly
how everything depended
        on her pulse in my fingertips
each exhale inhale
        nights my apnea would wake her
she would shake me awake
        restart my breathing

you refused to meet her
        talked of honour and shame
what you had learned over decades
        over continents
the passage of love
        what you had outlived
what will outlive us
        i had no words to convince you

# earliest memory (1)

the edge of a grove
where i would squat
fold arms over knees
and watch
the slow dance of fireflies
burn and fade


my hands skimmed long grass
in the hope that i would catch one
held cupped hands to my eye
peeked through the space between
thumb and index finger
for the promise of a green glow

# ghosts

they say that babbaji could measure truth
by the steadiness of a handshake
that a thief was once found out by an awkward twitch beneath shirt collar


when a body was found in the well –
it took three men to turn the crank
first the bucket
then the hand
twisted in the rope
the corpse dangled from one bloody wrist


the police came to our house
brought the body with them


babbaji touched the grey flesh
told not only the cause of death
(a severe beating, rope, and salt)
or how long since death
(two days)
but also those responsible
(family members – an uncle, a cousin)
and the reasons
(a dispute over land)

we were told to keep our distance from the well
that if we strayed too near
ghost hands would pull us in


we would hold pebbles
finger their smooth surface
and throw from a safe distance


the few ricochets
of stone against stone
and the long silence
before the splash
                    the echo


sometimes we would even dare to peek
the sky – a rippled blue moon in the dark hollow


and sometimes we would whisper into the well
await ghost voices to whisper back

shera was the blacksmith's son
shera because he feared nothing
on a dare one night
moonless and cold
wrapped a blanket around his shoulders
picked his father's hammer
an iron nail
and walked to a field
where decades earlier
a man had been nailed to the thick trunk of a tree
holes in his wrists and ankles


some said
that at night
you could still hear
the screams
of the crucified man


and when they found shera the next morning
his corpse held up by the blanket
which he had nailed to the tree
enveloped himself
and then struggled to get away


and now they say that it's shera's screams
you hear in that field at night

a place named for the morning mist that hangs over the river
or the nakoda who escaped under the cover of fog
or the buffalo still heard thundering when you put your ear to the soil


at a group retreat in kananaskis
we were asked to spend an hour alone
to reflect on our time together
to allow landscape to wash over us


i chose a spot on the river-bank
and watched clouds drift over devil's head
they moved so fast towards me
i had to steady my legs to keep from falling


what visited me was the image
of the lone lemon
on the one-branched tree
at the turner house
in the crags

the ghost child i once saw
in our house in london
sukhi removed and snapped a white nylon shirt in the dark
so we could both see the sparks
then hung the shirt on a hook on the door


and a young girl who took the shape of the fabric
crooked one finger
beckoned me


sukhi said it's only shadow

## earliest memory (2)

a kite festival
a sky filled with redgreenorange
diamonds and ribbon tails
strings tangled in strings
the sound of paper in wind


i held a plastic spool
aware of larger fingers folded over mine
yet convinced the measure of the world
was contained within my tiny hands

## circus

at the circus
the strongman lay down in front of the elephant
as two men placed a plank across his chest

the elephant walked slowly
picked an enormous leg in the air
placed his foot on the plank
the leg bent at a right angle
the strongman with his eyes closed
his muscles – knots upon knots


on the way home
the rains had flooded the road
and mohinderpal lifted me on his shoulders
the water first up to his waist
then his shoulders
the hesitation
the moment of decision
to turn back
or take another step forward

## magnesium glow

because it was the only place
in the school without windows
mister ellis took our class
to the assembly hall stage
drew thick velvet curtains
to complete the darkness


he threw a lit match onto a ribbon of magnesium
in a small asbestos dish


he wanted to teach us of flame and oxygen
to share with us the brightness of the world

# fuse

and in amritsar

           twins were born

  fused at the ankles

         their family

   refused the operation

       life as a constant

    three-legged race

      an unshakable shadow

     chachaji burned two candles

     side by side

      let the waxpools merge

     sliced a pomegranate

      down the middle

     but for the stem


     she said that's what it is

     two halves

     a common goal

    a sharing of seeds

     like should stick to like

      south asians with

      south asians

and i just stared at the light bulb filament

# fire-eater

sage held the camera to his left eye
looked at us with his right
               then click


and instead of portraits we got trees
instead of torsos we got feet
instead of flowers in tomkins park
we hit concrete


to know someone is to know the crucial ratio
between camper fluid flame and oxygen


when you felt the cool evaporation on your chin
you knew it was already too late
and soon your head and shoulders were in flames


so much changes between the ready and the click
the after-image clarity; happiness is no small gift

# proof

that one day
going to amritsar
the golden temple
sarinder tied a turban for me
white, in the *fojji* style
that pappaji was particular to
there was a pressure behind the ears
a heaviness i could not detach


as though that one day
in the end
at that final reckoning
the great judgement
as though that day in amritsar
would matter more than all others
those few hours more than the tens of thousands others


there is a photograph –
me walking backwards
down underwater steps
a kind of baptism
in holy water
a validation of heritage
                history –
naked shoulders
and arms holding a thick chain
the golden dome in the background

what it doesn't show is the large fish
teeming in the brown water
and that once in up to my chest
i felt a slap against my leg
and rushed out


later i paid a hundred *rupees* for a saffron sarong
a stainless steel tray
into which a *granthi's* apprentice
cupped steaming hot *prashad*
to lay in front of the *granth sahib*
an offering
a proof


i was in a long line
a congregation in waiting
on that thin path to the temple
water on both sides
loudspeakers boomed prayers
                    into the sticky afternoon air


i couldn't move
and became separated from my party

the thing is this –
the steel tray took the heat from the *prashad*
and became unbearable
i was completely surrounded
and held the tray above my head
small children scurried between our legs
some screaming for parents
who they could no longer see in the mass –
nobody seemed happy to be here
here, this most sacred of places
burning hands on stainless steel trays
as though in the end
on that final reckoning
what will matter are the scars of devotion

## rituals of bereavement

I

just hours after the body was recovered –
blue lips, eyes clear, skin washed clean
nails as white as kite string –
the professional mourners arrived
black veils, black robes
they beat their chests
broke bangles
wailed mourning songs


pappaji shouted at them
to take their circus elsewhere

II

the village we must visit
out of family duty
is built upon a hill
unable to navigate the narrow angled streets
sarinder parks the car on the main road


as we walk the last few hundred yards
my sister manjit teaches me
all these rituals of bereavement
                show up empty handed
                stay for chai but never dinner
                say the only things one can say at such times
                "it was her time"
                "god needed her back"
                biji's old phrase
                "no grief like that of a mother"


i learned the girl had died of a massive heart attack
sixteen, in her last year of school
and her father recorded messages onto audio-tapes
sealed them in bubble-wrap envelopes
sent them to her from england
this way she remembered his voice
and although they hadn't seen each other in years
they imagined this transaction closed distance

and on the last tape
he told her how proud he was of her
that the man they had chosen for her
was a good doctor
from a good family
the girl heard the familiar voice
then arranged the new tape
in a cardboard box beneath her bed

III

crosses and wreaths
on the side of highway two
driving north
north of didsbury


she said her earliest memory
was of the laundry room
in her grandfather's basement
rows and rows of flowers
hung upside down to dry
sometime after her grandmother's funeral


and for years her grandfather swept
dried petals stamen leaves
collected on the concrete floor

IV

back in herian
a woman who i called aunt
passed on unexpectedly
her body placed
on a thick block of ice
to await the arrival of her son from canada


her son, who i call cousin
arrived in delhi to discover that the rainy season had started early
had trouble finding a driver who would take him to herian
eventually he found someone but found the car had no windshield wipers
and the driver drove for hours with one hand on the steering wheel
the other arm bent through the side window
as he moved his hand up and down the windshield


soon the roads were so flooded and the rain so heavy that the car stalled
and my cousin hitched a ride in a transport company truck
huge eyes painted above the headlights
ganesh, guru nanak, a plastic jesus, and rosaries on the dash board


arrived in herian and had to wait two days
for the rain to subside so a funeral pyre would remain lit

he learned that being the eldest son
it was his duty to hold the torch
light the dry twigs
watched saffron flames consume saffron robes
bits of charred saffron cloth
rising into the matinal sky

V

at doctor naylor's funeral reception
maggie remarks
"thank god for mccinnis and holloway
without them would we know
how to grieve?"

# family

I

a young couple from copenhagen
showed up at our door
looking for the people
that lived there before
we moved in


for pappaji that was the essence of a man
                    *par admi da dil vada hauna chahida*
come in make yourself at home
stay as long as you please
a grandchild bouncing on his knee


one son sent to dara's food store
fresh okra and bittermelons
one to the butcher's for new zealand lamb
an older son to the off-license
johnny walker red label


the couple stayed for a week
and thirty years later
alongside photographs of their own family
keep a photograph of pappaji on their mantelpiece
their now-adult children having grown up
with stories of a stranger
who absolutely opened his home

II

the exercise was to draw a family portrait
and when pritpal arrived at parent-teacher interviews
the teacher acted rather concerned
of what conditions we might be living under


in this portrait
i had drawn not only my brothers, sister
sisters-in-law, nephews, nieces
but also anyone we called uncle or aunt
all my cousins
anyone from herian
the arshis and other neighbours on ellington road
dara from dara's food store
the lollipop man from kingsley road
the owners of the sweet shop


thirty-seven people in all –
the page filled with smiling faces
polyester pant-suits
flared trousers flowered shirts

III

sukhi's friend from senior school
turned out to be from the *pind* of biji's birth
and suddenly we had a new set of cousins
a new uncle and aunt
dinners back and forth
between the two households


and for the first time since pappaji's death
in biji's eyes
something like a look of recovery
of finding what she thought lost forever
in our new uncle's face

IV

born into a *jat sikh* family
that will marry only into other *jat sikh* families
to bear pure *jat sikh* children
who will marry only into other *jat sikh* families
to bear more *jat sikh* children who...

and i want to ask how pure is pure
and how far do we recede
and if the tracer stops at a hindumuslimparsi
a rickshaw driver or house cleaner
do we jump down the well
scurry under *manjas*
bury our heads, the soft earth by the *shupad*
emigrate to a new country
perform *sawa* to show others the purity of our hearts
to wear saffron only
grow our hair and stop shaving
do the *gurudwara* circuit
restrict our daughters to wearing *punjabi* suits, sorry no *saris*
justify future *jat sikh* marriages to dilute out the impurity
say well if someone wrote a satanic verses about sikhism
            never having read a book
well it's only been three hundred years...
swear to give up drinking for six months as atonement


or do we just not talk about it

and i want to remind of pure gold marriage *kara*
soft and pliable
bent from every knock on the steering wheel
every bang on the computer desk
every push on the garden shovel
every cup of chai delivered cold
every open hand closed hand
every whiskey tumbler through air
every body backwards through air
every twistturncontort
every wrong arrangement
every death bed apology
every alimony payment
every anti-depressant overdose
every pure gold *kara* sent back to the *sunaira* to have impurities added

# pineapple

harvey lived next door
that childhood house in england
his wife died and for a couple of years he lived alone


one year i brought him a harvest basket from school –
oranges, grapes, biscuits, tins of soup –
the term we used in those days was "old-aged pensioner"


a few days later as a thank you he gave me a large box of quality street chocolates


i'm not sure now whether he moved in with his son
or to an "old folks home"
but he sold the house and my brother mohinderpal bought it


in the attic we found harvey's old army gear –
a uniform, a straight razor, some medals
and a dissected hand grenade
a pineapple
a quarter chunk taken out


layers of green metal
a green hollow at its centre
it felt heavy in the hand
the way a limb heavy with sleep
might feel against a supporting palm

## earliest memory (3)

transparent plastic sandals
pappu's were green
and mine were blue


we would hold them to our eyes
convinced we had transformed the world
green birds in a green sky
blue oxen in a blue field

# fingertips

*kai jaga asian han, thusi sirf ek bar hi ja sakde ho*

saturday morning at the city pool
a woman i had loved over several months
tried to teach me to float – a matter of trust
to breathe underwater – like blowing out a candle she said


her family had welcomed me
with sunday dinners
a christmas sweater
weekends at the family cabin


we had shared so much
could anticipate moods and responses
cherished even moments of silence


that afternoon
the house empty
we lay down together
a faint smell of chlorine
on her hair
pink in her eyes
fingertips wrinkled

i had made up my mind
to break through the cultural double-life
quit this life of compartments
and was confident when i dialed the phone
the words easy and rehearsed
> *there is someone i would like you to meet*
> *could i bring her over tomorrow*


and on the other end
not silence
which i had expected
was prepared for
but vitriol
talk of betrayal and duty
disownment


i had no words to give back
no words in that childhood language
that mattered
and no words in my adopted language
that would be understood


i thought back to school
an assignment to measure heartbeat
and how exercise could affect it
the two fingers over the wrist –
the ten second count
then multiply by six

and my partner's heart-rate
the same after exercise as before
fingertips pressed against bone
calculated their own pulse

# II

✹

## surface

framed in a back-doorway
in summer rain
occasional lightning reveals their bodies


they both want to be changed somehow
want to bevel the awkward space
sway into each other
and speak new language


there is a close-up of raindrops
hitting hard on a wooden deck
then another of droplets
bouncing up to their ankles
then the close-up of an arm or a leg
a smooth surface becoming swollen


they have exhausted their stories
the ones left – they are not yet ready to share


the charcoal in a tube
in his brother's mouth


the squall that capsized
her mother's boat

54

they are still weighing each other
have not begun to question
difference or culture
family or duty
their hands have not begun to dismantle
what they have made
they long to continuously sink
into each other
with the perfection of glass birds


they know the stories that will push
towards a new membrane
a surface too thin to penetrate

## falter

where we falter is
we talk of love
too much
or too little


in sanjit's art
once occupied spaces
are shown empty


a spiral of shoes
well-worn and unpaired
all painted the same rust


his dead uncle's turbans
tied then pinned to a circular board
a colour for every occasion


and what we think of as empty space
now occupied


clay cupped between praying hands
then baked and scented with turmeric

she removes jewelry
at the bedside table
fingers ears wrists
silver by the night lamp


what i remember most clearly
is the shape of her mouth
the useless words that interrupt
perfect silence

## locust

the first to come to mind
is the one of locusts
and how the day turned into night

      your thumbs twist and lock
      your hands make wings
      that fly up to the night light
      the ceiling alive in shadow

a line of villagers
beat metal pots with wooden sticks
marched crop-heavy fields
so the locusts would not land

      your head on my stomach
      eyes closed
      hand flat in the hollow of my chest

the smell of newly cut mustard
a stillness that could choke
women moved flour sacks and pulses indoors
closed wooden slats over windows

*what we use to impress*
*is not always our own*
*a story heard so often*
*you take posession*


on your father's wedding day
the price tag on the lapel of his suit
and everyone too afraid or amused to tell him


you've only seen the photographs
that tell the story as though you were there

## mirror

in bertolucci's besieged
the camera loves
the mirror
the polished piano's black surface
or the slow movement
of music sheets blown by a breeze through an open window
or a soccer ball in a slow-motion bounce across the garden
how we resist then submit
dumb from the wait
how little we know ourselves
deny what we most desire
because we love the elusiveness
of what we think gives us purpose


we kissed in warm august rain
outside the plaza
large drops collected on earlobes and chins
rolled in our mouths like glass

## shadow

we jumped a fence
you convinced me to dive in
the pool's shallow end
me not knowing how to swim


i watched you and your shadow
meet on the water
left only surface and refraction
your body a pink blur against the blue tile
your shadow now enormous
swam beneath you


by the poolside
we held each other
eyes closed from the sting of chlorine
we laughed
shook from the laughing


the dark hair on my belly
flattened into a swirl
the cold tile and the night air
the swell of our bodies

on the drive back
you held the wheel
from the passenger side
while i cleaned my glasses

# ripple

overnight
a membrane of ice
had formed over the lake
and we bellied down on the dock
a child's red glove
floated on the surface


we reached down
pushed the ice gently
caused cracks
as sheet after sheet
drifted against then over each other
ice ripples
an echo in water


there was no one else around
and the air so cold
the plane thirty-thousand feet above
shook the dock with its noise

## tattoo

*the bride sent back*
*the marriage annulled*
*for the blue of a birthmark*
*or skin scarred smooth*
*hidden beneath clothes*
*to surface on the wedding night*


your body gave away so much of you
gave a way for hands
you wanted a tattoo –
with a pen
we drew the possibilities –
you stretched a leg towards the mirror
to see the paisley on your hip
i held another mirror behind you
the butterfly on your lower back

## splendour

and because we were unprepared
and because it was forbidden
we took shelter
from the street and the rain
in a concrete tunnel
in a school playground
where streetlights could not detect us


your hand reached back
angled my hardness to fit under


and when mouths and tongues could no longer continue
fingers pressed on vertebrae through cotton summer dress
your cheek hot against my shirt
your eyelash – a soft rhythm on my shoulder


we strive for fabric and texture
to relive the moment when for once
sense and senses
came together
we want some impossible permanence
not these arrivals and departures
not this ephemeral flutter

## trust

to fall here
you have to trust
the softness of snow
the enormity of sky


a winter morning in kananaskis
we walked a frozen river-bed
fresh snow over ice
under the ice flowing water
clear in the shade
green under sunlight


we stood still
our heavy boots silenced
listened to the soft trickle beneath
visible winter breath
the river's half hibernation


back at the hotel
so many layers
to unzip, unbutton, untie, unhook, unclasp, pull over
we collapsed
undone down our middles like cut fruit
bits of styrofoam –
that stippled ceiling –
snowed down on us
found the folds of our skins

## solstice

summer solstice on lesser slave lake
the midnight sun
a dim glow on the horizon
we watched long enough to turn to sunrise


you leaned against me
and your body numbed the places where we touched
insides of thighs
a shoulder


we awoke to the sound of swimmers
slapping water
and a grey morning rain
circles within circles
on the lake's dark surface

## mountain

crosses and wreaths
on the side of highway two


we played the game of earliest memory
to know each other through story
family history –
mountains framed by the kitchen window
in your grandmother's house
where she saved pennies in tin boxes
for a bus ticket to the city


the brilliant yellow of canola fields
an orange sunset over the mountains
and hawks perched on fenceposts

## summer-lines

yellow rectangle parachutes
against the greying sky
near beiseker


we parked to watch their slow descent
quiet and exact
onto an empty field


summer-lines on your face
your skin freckled
the air heavy with the promise of thunder


we could give ourselves away
with a gaze a little too long
distract or overcompensate for
the way our hands passed over each other

# detach

in the next room
the needle stuck
at the end of the record
our bodies moved in rhythm
with the static heartbeat
the crackle and thud


we knew each other's routines
favourite song lines and stories
passages from favourite books
underlined and read aloud
could read a stutter or awkward movement
into hesitation and insecurity


in the small hours
i walked an empty house
moonlit
cold slats of wood
a gentle lift of the needle
detach surface and sound

## notes on surface

because the flesh is a poor measure of time
does not flinch
can even imagine
the scrape the soft back of a hand
might have left
had it scraped at all
we choose third person narratives
and meld past relationships into one for their writing down


i could have chosen to say
that i was framed in the doorway
and the small body of a woman –
married then, now divorced –
leaned its weight against my shoulder
the rain had reawakened the smell of lilacs
her hair smelled faintly of chamomile
and her body after a long day –
a drive to the mountains
a walk around lake louise
a picnic of rye bread, green olives, piesporter –
felt heavier, more open than usual

there was no deck –
that house where i first learned love
as the marriage of pleasure and shame –
only a concrete step
from where the raindrops bounced
but not high enough
to touch us


the moist air gave us goosebumps
and we soon returned to a small bed in a basement bedroom
where we thought our entering would erase shadows
change us forever


it's the same woman
in the concrete tunnel
all our usual rooms unavailable
she said something of natalie wood
and splendour in the grass
a good title

# III

# pulse

the darkness reveals us

shapes without colour
shadows
negate difference

seven years
the amaryllis long dead
neglected in july heat

your mother's death
drew us together
then apart

is it enough
if all religion does
is give us
a way
to grieve

❋

to count each vertebra
to give each one
a place a year
a day


lightning flash through afternoon blinds


a prairie thunderstorm
the middle of summer

what if all we remember
are tears in a parking lot
a poem for your mother
a soaked summer dress
the Y of your arms


doors and windows
thrown open
dampness in doorways
and window frames


then sleep

your mother's ring
on a chain
around your neck


for that first year
you couldn't let go
driving speaking or eating
one hand at your throat
her pulse at your fingertips

a clothes dryer in the trees
a wardrobe in a dirt field
a yellow dining chair covered in snow
a red truck on its side


arion uses flashlights
in his night photography
creates patterns
that only the camera captures
the object out of place
the open shutter
full of motion
we never imagined

for all our talk of
change and adventure
we like our stasis


knees that fit the backs of your knees
arm over side, tucked beneath yours
feet touching heel to upper arch
my breath on your neck


          i knew a woman who travelled
          with the pillow from her bed
          the only way she could sleep
          in a hotel room or a friend's house
          and then the pillow was not enough
          and soon she gave up travelling altogether

we forgive those we love most easily
slurs and comments overlooked
afraid to lose familiarity


think infinitely well of yourself
not how someone you loved yesterday
is no longer in your life


no phone calls or chance meetings
it's agreed without mention
to not meet at the usual places


we forgive those we have loved
least easily

try hard to not remember
a child checks her brother's breathing in the night
a butterfly after a rainstorm caught in a drain


i loved you with
fingers and mouth
mouth then fingers

the music became background
backstage at south country fair
a purple summer sky
the grass cooled our bodies
the heartbeat in fingertips
stories from childhood
my years in another language
the gold ring from your mother
to my mother sorting
lentils from grit

how our capacities for detachment define us
how a hand over a hand can haunt for a lifetime

        sheri-d's grandmother in her nineties
        talks of a man she once met after the war
        "but my dance card was full dear"

        in an unconsummated marriage
        a woman sees her husband
        naked for the first time
        in an ICU bed
        after a suicide attempt
        they will have two children
        and she never sees him that naked again

and for others
an empty screen
a wordless page
no memory of the pulse in another's skin
or laughter in a closed room

a wet instep on a concrete floor

the arc of a figure skater
circling on one leg
head twisted back
a sparkler in each hand


in the photograph becomes
yellow hoops of light
entrapping a ghost

only a childhood language
can describe
childhood memories
and even then…


rain was not rain
but *minh*
the english *minh*
awakens fragrances
the scents of flowers
the smell of hot concrete after a summer downpour
"mom" – the old woman who lived at number four
who everyone called "mom" –
drenched in a storm
being led indoors by "dad"
her clenched hands
still convinced that her home
lay on our side of the fence

that childhood language
cannot describe
how someone enters your life
completely
then leaves

lilac petals on the ground
the promise of rain in the air

you turned around
placed me hard between your legs
stroked you/me in the mirror


finger comb your hair


you always dressed too soon
running from or running to

# IV

*for lucy and libby turner*
*for roy miki*

## earliest memory (4)

a sandstone cliff-wall
pockmarked by wind and monsoons –
a pomegranate sliced and sucked dry –
and in every pockmark
a monkey
toy faces / monkey chatter


i sat in a basket
on the handlebars
of my sister's bicycle
and my legs dangled and shook

# the crags, somewhere near mittagong, n.s.w.

The people who lived here before us / also loved these high mountain meadows…
— Robert Hass

You are of it / and you are not, / and you know that very clearly
— Roy Kiyooka via Roy Miki

then this morning in the valley
below the turner house
chestnut horses
suck the dew off winter grass
and a cloud
beyond the first row of eucalyptus
above the creek
shifted side to side
refused to lift
even when the sun
began its slow creep
over the meadow


yesterday at dusk –
lucy says it's the best time to see them –
kangaroos, laughing kookaburras
the clichés of australia
come alive

and a tree grown to split a large rock
separating the now-two-halves
further year by year


a lemon tree grown too large
for the plant pot that once contained it
the roots growing through the cracked clay
finding more ground to grow into
a lone lemon on a lone branch


volkswagens and ford trucks
dumped in a ditch
all moss and rust


they call this place the crags
for the sandstone cliff-wall
pockmarked by weather


there are still remnants of the people who lived here before
a flat stone in the ground
where tools and weapons were sharpened
three smooth divots like footprints

last night as we talked of "human wishes"
lucy placed a square block of huon pine in her lap
unfurled her apron of new-moon chisels
and with precise movements of her wrist
she extracted curled slivers
the smell of pine
the sound of sharp metal through wood
until a woman's face appeared
slight nose, small mouth
hair in coils on the sides of her head
she must have felt it
the pulse in the grain
the face in that blank wood
or at least realized the potential


lucy says each sliver is a decision
and what's left is the face
and decisions around her feet


back in calgary there is someone
i imagine i could love
because of the hair that falls over one eye
how her hands distract my body
we've shared stories in the half-light of early morning
and think this intimate knowledge
can translate to something indelible – of undeniable worth

her voice changes when she speaks of the incident with the train
the moment of clarity before the collision
how by all regards she should not be here
we've twinned around each other and swallowed
the biology of comfort
at times we talk over telephones
and believe we have negated distance


we fake a level of intimacy
our few months alliance cannot bear
not knowing we have joined a narrative
opened a book mid-way and become characters


history is the poor memory of an old man
who cannot remember if it rained on his wedding day
where he was for the birth of his first child
a man who tries a door and finds it locked
and then tries it again anyway


lucy and i are searching for a cave
a cave with ancient drawings
i imagine hunting scenes –
the prey and the kill –
for that is what we are taught
of ancient cave drawings

some say it's a hoax
some local teenagers' idea of a joke
and some suggest a visit by those whose ancestors lived here
the suggestion voted down by local council


still searching for that cave –
lucy remarks that when a child
she was the best at finding it –
seventy yards up a steep slope
behind a thicket of bushes
but the cave seems to shift
and sometimes alludes her


we search for an hour
and then return to the turner house

# earliest memory (5)

a sandstone cliff-wall
pockmarked by wind and monsoons
and in every pockmark a parrot
bluegreenyellow

i sat in a basket
on the handlebars
of my sister's bicycle
lifted my hands
placed them over my ears
frightened by the echoes
within that cliff-wall

# the crags - reprise

on july 1st
a display of fireworks
to honour the canadian contingent
the sky above north wollongong beach lit up
as we huddle for warmth


we feel a connection to this celebration of home
and for a while
forget the language
heard earlier that day
the story of six-hundred fujianese migrants
risking all for dreams we have sold them


history teaches us nothing
and what we see as clearly wrong in the past
we fail to see in the present
and our newspapers simply state again
                              go home

V

※

## calcutta

we flew in
from separate continents
met on sudder street
in a hotel
where shashi kapoor and jennifer kendall
often stayed
or so the photographs
in the stairway
would have us believe


second/third generation servants
white gloved, waxed moustaches
feather fans on their turbans
serve yorkshire puddings
 custard pies
to third/fourth generation imperialists
 "oh, the children
 the big brown eyes
 their dark hair –
 they are so lovely"


a jet-lagged first afternoon
we lay together as strangers
geckoes on the ceiling
bollywood song videos on the small television
the sound muted

we fell asleep
and awoke to the sound of a political rally
the amplified speech filling our room
    "the necessities –
    clean water
    safety on the streets
    basic education for our children"


as you measured drops of lavender oil
into the claw foot tub
we knew we had undressed too soon
and stood in the steam
unsure hands dangled awkwardly at our sides

in the tub we sat on opposite ends
and bathed each other like children
offering tired arms
to have them soaped and rinsed clean


if we could only recover
the promise of poems
and how i grew soft
once inside you

## grace

*for helen flavell*

I

what we choose
        what the world chooses for us
four men stand waist-deep
        a few steps down *mir ghat*
in the sacred river ganges
        their *kodthas* flower around them


in their hands they hold shallow straw baskets
        which they swirl on the river's surface
to sift the river's sediment
        of mud ash and bone


what the river would make its own
        for all we leave behind
bits of jewelry –
        a wedding band, a gold or silver tooth –
anything that will not surrender
        to the heat of the funeral pyre
anything too precious
        and not precious enough

it is dawn and these four men
        so intent on their work
seem oblivious
        to the thousands of bathers around them
thousands immersed
        in the thick brown *amrith*


most have travelled days
        for what grace this murky entrance will glean
what grace the lighting of *diwas*
        the whispering of prayers will grant them


water thick from the waste
        of the once imperial city
where swimmers come up for air
        spit what they have swallowed
children playing games of chase
        dive into the thickness


groups of women
        make curtains of wet *saris*
behind which other women
        wash their bodies
tall shadows
        impressed upon the fabric

the infirm and the very young
        are carried in
floated on the surface
        the river closing its liquid hands over them


*sadhus* cup water
        into joined hands
hold them in prayer
        as the water slips back into the wide ganges


on the opposite bank
        the sun battles the morning haze
a few camels, a bank of trees
        and beyond that nothing


it was also the time of the morning pyres
        corpses wrapped in white cotton
sprinkled with jasmine buds
        afloat on beds of dried branches
eldest sons holding torches
        bent arms, lowered heads


because we wished to respect
        the privacy of grief
we tried to look away
        and could not look away

II

sparrows drunk on berries
        flew into the glass
of your kitchen window
        your childhood home
late summer you would find one
        dazed on the lawn


your mother would cup her hand
        around the delicate body
angle the beak into a thimble of whisky
        just enough
until the pressure of wings against her palm
        informed her she could let go

III

it was shortly after we boarded the bus in putna
that we saw it
(at the same time?)
you at the front of the bus
shane and i further back
it was dawn and after two days of travel from darjeeling
we were numb to everything
and at the moment i saw it
i thought nothing


you at the front of the bus
in the ladies section
close to the driver
i was hoping you hadn't seen it
that the luggage and the driver's seat
obscured your sightline
that you hadn't seen the corpse on the road
a corpse of a man – naked from the waist down
fresh
the guts spilt out – all genitals and gut
from the impact of what had struck him
and people stood around
dazed with sleep
scratching heads
wondering what to do
with the untouchable body
what rituals there might be for this

it was days before we mentioned it
days before in mid-conversation
one of us – i can't remember who –
stuttered "did you see?"
knew that the answer we wanted
was the comfort of common experience

.

IV

what is it we would like to contain
            in our hands
impress upon our bodies
            in a rooftop hotel
where you balanced your body
            on top of mine
so that no part of you touched the bed –
            arms spread wide
your breath on my neck –
            to absorb families and pasts
sink into each other
            to learn to float


one night a wind-storm blew the shutters open
            i saw the rooftop sleepers
huddled in corners
            blankets wrapped around shoulders
waiting for an end
            empty rope beds in the rain

what was the dream of the unified field
        what did we mistake it for
photographs in a wallet
        a story essential
what those particular moments
        we moulded our lives around held for us
capacities for desire, denial, fulfillment
        what we had used as protection
all our lives from what we most wanted
        and most resisted


what happened
        what we think happened
what we were told
        what we told each other later
how we wrote it down
        what the photograph shows

# Acknowledgements

Ashok Mathur and Paulo da Costa are owed much for their keen editorial skills.

The friendship, inspiration, council and/or reward of the following needs to be noted: Richard Harrison, Phinder Dulai, Shane Rhodes, Peter McPhee, Louise Bak, Arion Predika, Derrick VanderVliet, Writers for Change, Calgary WordFest, *filling Station*, Sage Theatre, the TarDisaster Project, Leadership Calgary, TSAR, Canada Council, Alberta Foundation for the Arts, the Writers Guild of Alberta, *fast forward*.

Thank you to Blaine Kyllo and Brian Lam at Arsenal Pulp Press.

The following were constant companions during the writing of this book:

| | |
|---|---|
| Anne Carson | *Plainwater* |
| Cat Power | *Moon Pix* |
| Jorie Graham | *The Dream of the Unified Field* |
| | *The End of Beauty* |
| Robert Hass | *Human Wishes* |
| | *Sun Under Wood* |
| Joe Henry | *Fuse* |
| Smog | *Red Apple Falls* |
| Songs: Ohia | *Ghost Tropic* |
| Lucinda Williams | *Essence* |

Some of these poems have appeared in: *West Coast Line*, *filling Station*, *Alberta Views*, *Babel*, *Dandelion*, *The Capilano Review*.